Th...

Versie's unique approach will inspire you to reach your dreams. This practical roadmap for success in business and in life will leave you feeling inspired, encouraged and empowered. It is a must read for those just starting their careers as well as an excellent desk reference for every career or business person.
**Carolyn Fleming Hugley, Georgia State Representative
House District 113**

Read this book- it will help you determine your destiny by allowing you to choose the right shoes.
**Dan Copeland, President/CEO, Copeland & Associates
2001 Named Top Lobbyist in State of Georgia**

Choose Your Shoes...Then Take a Walk is a "to do" list for living a rewarding and productive life. It is filled with common sense wisdom and encourages the reader to participate in life.
Phil Parker, Speaker and Author of *Kiss Yourself Hello!*

Versie's commonsense, real-life approach is both refreshing and uplifting. It's time to get back to the basics.
Lisa A. Wolf, Senior Vice President , Elliot Executive Source

Anyone entering the work force should read this book. It contains both practical and timeless truth about relationships and business common sense.
Scott MacLellan, CEO Foodbuy, LLC, Author, *Amanda's Gift*

Choose Your Shoes...Then Take a Walk is refreshing and inspiring at a time when Business and our Society in general need a positive lift in spirit.
William Raaths, CEO Great Northern Corp, Appleton, WI

A great book! Reading it was like revisiting an old friend and sharing words of wisdom. Versie's journey will make it easier for others who will come along the same path.
Willa Brigham , Author, *Stinky Johnson and Other Tales*

Don't underestimate the impact that this slim, easy to read book can offer! Versie's lessons and ideas in *Choose Your Shoes...Then Take a Walk* are perfect whenever you feel like a bit of inspiration.
Bonnie Ross-Parker , Author, *Walk In My Boots ~The Joy of Connecting*

Versie gives us a view into her approach to life. She has a tremendous understanding and love of people and life. I thoroughly enjoyed her boldness and honest words.
Dave Pierro, Team Leader, Alta Resources

Versie is an expert in seeing the options in life as well as in business, and I'm delighted that she's decided to share her view of the world in this book..... (About time!)
Joanne Shufelt, Vice President, Sales North American Commercial Business Georgia-Pacific Corporation

Choose Your Shoes... Then Take a Walk is great advice for successful career management.
Audrey B. LeGrand, Certified MasterStream Instructor

Choose Your Shoes... Then Take a Walk, a book of great substance with a sense of humor that does not diminish the seriousness of the issues.
Marjorie H. Young, Commissioner Georgia Merit System

Exceptional! An extremely positive account of a black female's progression through the ranks of corporate sales. Versie's account of her journey and strategy for dealing with opposition and roadblocks is testament to what we can accomplish once we decide on the pair of shoes we wish to wear, and how far we wish to walk in them.
Jan J. Williams, Estate Planning Specialist, AXA Advisors

As a young woman, I found *Choose Your Shoes...Then Take a Walk* as a must read if you are planning to climb up the corporate ladder, or become an entrepreneur in the business world. This book is insightful and thought provoking.
Madinah S. Ali, President/CEO, MSA Global Advisory Group

Choose Your Shoes... Then Take a Walk

Empowering Personal
and Professional
Success Ideas
for Your Journey

by
Versie M. Black

Versie Consulting
Atlanta, Georgia

For book orders, author appearance inquiries and interviews, please contact the author via website at:

www.VersieConsulting.com or by mail at:

Versie Consulting
P.O. Box 724495
Atlanta, Georgia 31139

Cover design: Doing80.com
Interior design: Doing80.com
Author's photograph:
Sawyer Photography Studio, Marietta, GA

Library of Congress Cataloguing In Publication

ISBN 0-9729138-0-7
(Trade paperback $12.95)

My sincere thanks to:

My pastor & spiritual leader,
Rev. Dr. Walter L. Kimbrough,
Senior Pastor of
Cascade United Methodist Church
Atlanta, Georgia,
who told me I must write this book.

Ethel Foster, Jacqueline C. Gholson,
Marquita Harris Void and
Sarah Adams Yeary,
my dear friends, for reviewing this book.
Gracie Hunter White and Anna Wilson
for proofreading and critiquing the text.

All of my friends who took the time to
respond to my request for inspiring
business philosophies and comments
for this book.

And to all the people who said, "Go For It!"

Dedication

This is dedicated to my mother, Bertha Louise Black, who has been my constant supporter and taught me early in life that all dreams are possible.

To my daughter, Valerie, who is still searching for her dreams; "If you can dream it, you can achieve it."

I thank God for all of my blessings, my sense of humor, and for giving me the talent to write this book.

Table of Contents

Preface

On most occasions, men wear either black or brown shoes. Women, on the other hand, choose shoes based upon the occasion, the dress code, the season, or the outfit.

Sometimes the shoes are flats, sometimes the shoes are high heels and other times the shoes are mid-heel. Sometimes the shoes are dressy suede, sometimes the shoes are sling back, sometimes the shoes are slides and there are times when the shoes are mules. Sometimes the shoes are open toe, sometimes the shoes are sandals, sometimes the shoes are pumps, sometimes....

Unlike men in business, women have to navigate to different rules. Unlike men in the business arena, who have lots of mentors, women have a smaller field of mentors from whom to seek guidance. Unlike all of the aforementioned, African American women and people of color have fewer mentors and fewer shoes.

This book is written in the hope that it will help others regardless of gender, race, profession, culture or ethnicity to navigate the rough waters of business, offer quicker insight into the maze of life and appreciate the humor in their daily surroundings.   This book also reflects some of my experiences and my philosophy of living.

If one person can use one point from what I share here to help propel them to the next level, then it will have been a good day and I will be pleased. This is not a blueprint for success; it is merely a collection of some of the tips I have learned on my journey and the shoes I have chosen.

Versie M. Black
Atlanta, Georgia
October, 2002

"We cannot control what other people do or say; so therefore go with your own convictions and make the Good Lord a part of your plan."

Curt Gentry
NFL Chicago Bears

Learn Their Sports

Lucky for me, I like sports and grew up with three brothers and male cousins who played sports and who taught me the rules of the games very early.

When they would finally let me play with them, they never gave me any advantages because I was a girl. In fact, my older brother pushed me harder because of my gender, and for that I thank him. Most of the time when men give examples, they use words, phrases and descriptions associated with sports. They say things like, "tee it up," "home run," "4th and 10," "step up to the plate," "the ball is in your court," "slam dunk," "fast break," "break away," "jump ball," and "home stretch." Since this terminology is what most men understand, it is to our advantage when women understand some facets of sports.

To help myself prepare, I would read the sports section of the newspaper so I would know the latest sport topics and subjects of the day. I would remember who was in first place in the leagues (National League or American League), results of key games, key players and what they did recently, and some major plays and statistics. Most men usually relax when you engage them in conversation about their favorite teams, players, theories, etc. Using this strategy has proven to be one of the safest and quickest ways for women to get men interested enough to hear what women have to say. Many times men equate women as being "okay" if we know or care about their games.

I have also done a few things that impress men about sports. I've made it a personal goal to attend games at all of the National Football League stadiums in the USA. I am in the process of completing my goal, and as I write this book, I have only four of the old stadiums (those built before 1999) left to visit. I will begin another quest to go to a game in the new stadiums. My friends tease me saying that I will be 82 years old and still loving sports and going to different sporting events. The reaction of my friends and customers is most interesting regarding my goal to visit all of the National Football League stadiums. Those who are aware of my desire to visit these stadiums still call and offer me tickets to games at the stadiums I have yet to visit.

I feel honored that so many people are sensitive to my dream and want to help me accomplish this goal. I also make it a point to go to baseball stadiums, basketball arenas, and hockey games. I have gone to the Masters, the Doral Open, and other major golf events. Occasionally, I play in charity golf tournaments. This gives me exposure, additional networking opportunities, and a more knowledgeable understanding of the games.

I went to a NASCAR-Winston series event with a customer who truly loves NASCAR. This elevated my relationship with the customer. We spent the day bonding. He shared his knowledge of the sport and I learned something new. It expanded my understanding of a sport that I knew nothing about and I gained an appreciation for the thrill that the fans experience for their heroes in the NASCAR. The best part of these activities was knowing I did them for my personal benefit and not to impress anyone else.

In 1986, I was the first woman at Wisconsin Tissue to qualify to join the Million-Dollar Club. This was an elite club where Sales people had to reach their sales goals, have a minimum increase of 20% from the prior year, and meet other criteria. When I started with the company in 1980 and attended the first National Sales Meeting in 1981, I witnessed a select group of guys being inducted into this club and each receiving a ring. Inspired by their achievement and recognition, I set a personal goal, namely, "I am going to get one of those rings and be part of the Million-Dollar Club."

We were at our 1987 National Sales meeting and I learned that I was playing golf for my recreational activity. Now normally, I would have signed up for sightseeing, going to the spa, hanging by the pool or another form of relaxing. I asked who signed me up for golf and I learned that not only did the president sign me up but he also put me on his team. I took that as a sign that just maybe I should try this.

I explained to the president I did not know how to play golf and he said he understood that. This guy was an avid golfer with a 2 handicap. He took me aside and said, "If you want to be successful in this business, it would be to your advantage to learn something about the game." Therefore, I learned something about golf. I took a few lessons, and now when men and women ask me if I play golf, my initial response is, "Yes, but not too well." I go out and give it my best. I know I will never be Nancy Lopez, Annika Sorenstam, Cristie Kerr or Rachel Teske. Some days I play better than others, but playing golf is so much fun.

I was playing with a very good golfer (8 handicap) for the first time. I got up to the tee on the first hole and I had a bad drive. I finished the hole with a double bogey. On the second hole, I teed off badly again. The golfer told me to take a mulligan. I said, "No, I want to take all my strokes so I can see how I play on this course." The third hole was a par 4, which I pared. I told the golfer, "Accident." The fourth hole was a par three. I got a birdie and I said to the golfer, "Luck". However, I noticed that after the fourth hole, the golfer no longer suggested for me to take a mulligan, but he had begun to count my strokes.

I learned to play golf to have more time with clients and to be part of the team. Now, I thoroughly enjoy the sport and it has served me well.

Learn their games.

"If you're going to play the game properly, you'd better know every rule."
-Barbara Jordan

"As a mathematician and insurance underwriter, my experience and success have been in my strength of risk taking and negotiation. Risk is the avenue for finding answers/solutions different from the norm. Without it, you'll always get what you always got."

Revaple Thomas McNair
Underwriting Manager
AETNA, Inc.
Alpharetta, GA

Risk

Take the attitude that *if it is to be, it is up to me.* Do not leave it up to others to fight the battles. (Now you see, I am using terminology that men often use - battle, war). Do not leave it up to others to make the point or to promote a cause.

About twenty-two years ago, I began to work for a very reputable company. I noticed that I was the only female in outside sales. When I asked management about it, I was informed they were looking for qualified females and had every intention of changing the dynamics of the sales field. Six months after I started, ten additional women were hired for outside sales. At this point we were eleven strong. I thought okay, management was true to their commitment to change the landscape of the sales team. Four to six months later, two more women were hired. Management continued to hire women for outside sales. After one year, one of the females left the company and she was replaced with a male. When another female left the company she was replaced with a male also. This practice of replacing each woman with a male was reducing the number of women and we were slowly losing ground in our total. I went to a key management person and asked why they replaced these two women with men. His response was the women did not work out. I said, "Help me understand this. The women did not work out, therefore you needed to replace them with men?" "Yes", he replied. "When men do not work out who do you replace them with?", I asked.

Looking back, I realize I was bold in questioning established practices, however, I felt I needed to get management to take another view. They replaced men with men and women with men. It was not as if they replaced men with elephants, lions, or something else.

Management of this company needed to see that if they allowed men to have other factors, not just gender as to why they do not stay, or why they leave, then they need to allow the same factors and differences for women. We have to point out that, unlike what the fashion industry would have us believe about women, one size does not fit all. Sometimes we have to take a stand. Take the attitude that, *if it is to be, it's up to me.*

At one time, we had too many sales people in the same city, but instead of eliminating a sales person we wanted to try and keep all of the sales representatives. A few months later, an opportunity arose for one of the representatives to relocate to a new territory. This particular sales representative had expressed a desire to relocate because he wanted to remain with the company. Although it was his idea to relocate, he had "hemmed and hawed" for a few months with his manager about the move, so I got involved. I could tell that he was uncomfortable with the relocation, but I needed to hear him say it. During the phone conversation, I questioned him to identify the issues he felt needed to be resolved before he made the move. He shared the following concerns: he did not know the area; he did not know a lot of people in the new area; and he was not sure that he would like his new surroundings. He felt he would make unwise decisions with the customers and that he would not be able to function well in this new arena.

First, in light of these uncertainties, he wanted assurance and a guarantee that if he did not like the new area, I would relocate him back to the city where he currently resided. Secondly, he wanted to be paid more money because he did not know the customers and the products for these customers in the new area. He said he was sure he would make dumb decisions, and he would feel better making these decisions if he was better compensated. Thirdly, I must guarantee that he will be successful in his new territory. Never once did he tell me he needed and wanted training on the products and a clearer understanding of the customer. Moreover, never once did he sound enthusiastic about the opportunity. Based upon our discussion, I decided not to relocate him because I sensed he was not ready to take the risk. He wanted me to guarantee his success.

No one can guarantee your success. If the drive for risk is not truly part of your desire, you will not be happy and you will not do a good job. If the possibility of success does not energize, excite and motivate you, the reality of failure will creep into your conscience. There are no guarantees in life. If you are truly looking for guarantees, you should not get out of bed.

All you can do is to give your best, because guarantees are not part of the program or the curriculum.

"Anyone who has never made a mistake has never tried anything new."
-Albert Einstein

"There is no security in life, only opportunity."
-Mark Twain

"Set your goals, critique periodically and be flexible to change to achieve maximum success."

Jacqueline C. Gholson
District School Social Worker
Shaker Heights City School District
Shaker Heights, OH

Plan

You need to have a plan. Write it down and refer to it often to see if you are on track as you monitor your plan to chart your progress.

The plan will probably change or need adjustments over time due to various circumstances. You won't leave home on a journey without a map or a plan; therefore, you should not start a career without a plan. The adjustments are like traveling— sometimes you will take an interstate and other times you will take the side streets. Share your plan with others who you trust; people who can offer insight and constructive feedback to your idea.

In navigating your course you may have to zig and zag. Plans do not always travel in a straight line. You need to be willing to take lateral moves or downgrade to get experience in all departments. In 1989, I was promoted to National and Group Account Manager and relocated to Atlanta. During the interview for this position, a manager asked me if I would take the job if I knew it would be changing the next year to Assistant Regional Manager instead of National and Group Accounts. "Yes I would still take the job," I said. I accepted the position and the challenge. I worked one year in the National and

Group Accounts position; then two years as Assistant Regional Manager, before I went back to National Accounts.

In 1993, after working four years in these various positions, I was promoted to Regional Manager and relocated to Kansas City. Four years later, I took another lateral move as Regional Manager and relocated to Chicago. Some co-workers asked, "Why would you make another lateral move?" I took another lateral move because the region was larger and it gave me another opportunity to get to know more customers and a chance to work in a different environment.

I am glad I took the different positions in various regions of the country. Being involved with diverse customers throughout North America, working with the various Marketing and Buying Groups, and National and Corporate Accounts, moving and changing jobs helped me become a candidate for the position as Director of Sales for Georgia Pacific Tissue.

You must have a plan. Take a look at your company's organizational chart and think about what you want to do long term. Be realistic about your time frame. Talk to the persons in those departments and divisions to gain an understanding of what they do, how they feel about what they do, and what they see as the vision and long term plans. Look at who is being promoted and find out what is unique about their work and work habits. Listen and notice when there are changes in the areas where you want to work. Example: A woman heard that a person was retiring in the department where she wanted to transfer. She began to research and determine what she needed to know to get an interview and ultimately the promotion.

Review your skills to learn and identify what you will need to do to be promoted or transferred to these business units. Keep in mind as you are planning your career strategy, not to discuss all of your plans with those who cannot make a difference. Neither would it be in your best interest to share your plans with those who have no influence, authority, or the ability to help you. Silence is more than golden; it is platinum.

If there are other companies or other career avenues you want to pursue then you should also review those companies and venues. Investigate what they do and determine what type of people they are looking to hire for their team. Review their track record and try to get an understanding of their goals, plans and future directions.

Planning is essential to all phases of our lives. I am often perplexed as to how families can get together for funerals or other emergencies. However, these same members cannot or will not plan for pleasant events. They will say that two years, one year, six months or whatever the time frame in the future is too far away for them to think and plan that far in advance. No one knows what the future holds; hence we should plan anyway. If you have to make adjustments, so be it!

"People who fail to plan, plan to fail. Plan your work and work your plan."
-Anonymous

"The time to repair the roof is when the sun is shining."
-John F. Kennedy

"Nothing happens until you write it down. Put your vision in writing in order to communicate to others what you hope to accomplish."

Gerald A. Fernandez
President
Multicultural Foodservice
& Hospitality Alliance (MFHA)
Providence, RI

Document

Keep a journal of the many things you do throughout your career. Document your accomplishments as they occur so you do not have to rely on your memory months or years later.

The best time to gauge the accuracy of events and accomplishments is when they are occurring since accomplishments, successes, and events tend to get fuzzy over time. Document the situation, the task, and the results. Recap the role you played in the situation, how you felt, and what you will do differently the next time. Give documentation your proper attention and do not minimize the job or the results.

Translate the accomplishments into skills used and not just tasks or projects completed. Make sure the key people know what you have done and get feedback as to how you can improve your performance. On the other hand, remember there is an element of tact and diplomacy that goes along with getting the key people to see your contributions. Request feedback from your managers and challenge them to give you progress reports. Make a self-assessment as well as a formal career assessment to determine your skills and level of competency. Ask, request and insist upon access to the type of tools needed to improve your skills. Inquire regularly about seminars and other opportunities where you can participate to improve, refresh or enhance your skills.

Documentation helps when you are working with new employees, new peers and new team members who may not know you and who may have allegiance to someone else. When I began working with a new company, I had a customer service representative who constantly questioned everything I asked her to do. Often she would tell me that I had not asked her to do the things we were discussing. This was untrue. I knew I needed her on my side in order for me to be successful because she was familiar with the procedures and the customers. Rather than tell her she was wrong and cause her to become defensive, I used a non-threatening approach to let her know I clearly remembered the date and time I requested something of her. Each time I made a request, I began our conversation by telling her the date and the time of our last meeting.

In a short time, she realized my ability to recall dates and situations was credible and real. She began to make a joke when we discussed an issue in question. "What were you wearing when you made the request?", she asked. To her surprise, most times, I could tell her not only what I was wearing, I was able to repeat the conversation word-for-word, restating what each of us had said. This newly—developed respect and relationship helped us become a great team. Rarely did my customer service representative question me about dates, time or circumstances after that.

After a major meeting, several of us were debriefing to try to determine the direction we should proceed. At one point in the debriefing, I told my teammates exactly where each person was sitting around the table and the order in which they had spoken. The key to help me with recalling facts is documenting. As time passes the memory will fade, and you never know when you will need to produce valid information.

Documentation is paramount when you are pursuing opportunities when facts need to be confirmed. Documentation and facts eliminate guess work, helping the scorecard to be concrete, factual, and void of emotions, generalities, and perceptions.

"Facts do not cease to exist because they are ignored."
- Aldous Huxley

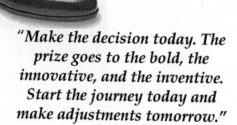

"Make the decision today. The prize goes to the bold, the innovative, and the inventive. Start the journey today and make adjustments tomorrow."

Alexander Black, Jr
President
Black Technology Corp
Dayton, OH

Make Decisions

Do not wait for everything to be perfect before you make a decision. Anyone can be a Monday morning quarterback. In reality, the game is usually played on Sunday afternoon, and the decision has to be made when it is 4th down and 20, the ball is on the 49 yard line and there is 1:20 left in the game. You cannot affect change from the sideline. You have to be in the game to win.

Make decisions. Most often, doing nothing is not an option. If you do not make the decision, it may be made for you. Do not under any circumstance give up your right to make a decision. If you do, in the final analysis, you will be the one who has to suffer the consequence. I have found that most people appreciate a decision made, particularly, when it is made in a timely manner. When the decision is not a pleasant one, the quicker it is made, the easier it is for the recipient to accept. When you procrastinate because you don't want to be the bearer of bad news, you actually exacerbate the problem and place your credibility in question. You do not gain points when you procrastinate and fail to give a timely answer.

A manager once asked me to give my approval for a program he wanted for a client. I thought the program was excessive, and I asked him to explain why we needed to do this. He proceeded to give me the rationale as to why I should support this request. After much discussion, I decided to go with his suggestions and I supported his decision for the program because he was closer to the customer. The very next day, he sent me three e-mails telling me he did not want to do this anymore. He began to second guess himself. I was perplexed because he had put so much time into selling me on the idea. I had noticed this was not the first time he had been given the okay to proceed only to have him rescind on his idea or not follow up. His style was one of "fear" in making a decision and he wanted others to make the decision for him. I say, make the decision, for it is better to ask for forgiveness than to ask for permission. My asking for forgiveness far outweighs my asking for permission 10-to-1.

Enter the premise with the understanding that the decision will be successful, however, the decision may fail. Sometimes you have to make the decision with 70% of the information. Make the decision with the information you have, not what you hope to get next week. Sure, some of the decisions you make will not necessarily be the best decisions, but let's hope the good ones outweigh the bad ones. One thing is for sure, just like you cannot "hit a home run" if you never step up to bat, not making a decision is not a good option.

Put the decision that needs to be made in perspective. I was visiting a friend and she was trying to decide where we should go for dinner. "What do you feel like eating", she pleasantly asked. I told her that except for a few foods I was allergic to, I was flexible as to where we had dinner. She proceeded to give me a choice of restaurants. After she named about five restaurants, I firmly told her to pick one because this was her city and I had no idea which restaurant was best based upon locations, food choices or services. She went to great lengths to get me to decide. Making a decision has never been one of my shortcomings. I said, "We are going to the restaurant that is closest to where we are right now. It is getting late and if we do not like our choice of restaurants, we can always leave and go someplace else." Besides, how difficult can it be? We would have the opportunity to eat again in about 12 hours. Make a decision.

Most of the decisions that need to be made are not monumental. I was visiting another friend who wanted to know what kind of cold cereal I liked for breakfast. I gave her a list of three and told her any one of these three cereals would be fine. The next day, she brought home two cereals because she could not decide which one I really wanted. This is the ultimate in not making a decision because I had told her any one would be a good choice.

On one occasion I asked my assistant to make one change on a document and then send it to the recipient. I was perplexed when she came back to get me to check the document once more. I asked her if she had made the change and she said yes. "Why are you giving this to me again?" I asked. "I wanted to be sure you meant for me to send it," she said. Make a decision.

"In any moment of decision the best thing you can do is the right thing, the next best thing is the wrong thing, and the worse thing you can do is to do nothing."
-Theodore Roosevelt

"It is common sense to take a method and try it. If it fails, admit it frankly and try another. But, above all, try something."
Franklin D. Roosevelt

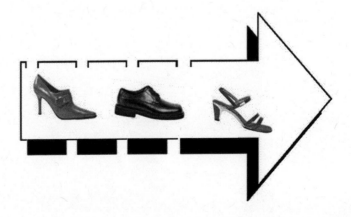

"To be successful in the fullest sense of the word, a woman must establish her priorities between family, work, friends, community, and religion. Every day those priorities are tested, if you are an executive woman. Every day, one must be congruent with those priorities to be truly happy and successful in the long run."

Meredith Reuben,
CEO
Eastern Bag and Paper Group
Milford, CT

Prioritize

There are only 24 hours in a day. I am not, nor do I want to be super woman, wonder woman, or magical woman. In prioritizing the tasks, sort them into categories of A, B, & C, with A's being the most important, B's the next important, and C's the least important. Do the A's, then the B's. The C's have a tendency to be taken care of in the long run with minimum effort or the tasks cease to be important and will not need to be done.

You should review your list from time to time because circumstances will cause your list and priorities to change. If you find that you cannot keep up with your responsibilities, if the work begins to control you, or if it takes an enormous amount of time to do the job, you either need help, more people, or maybe you do not have the tools and skills necessary to perform the tasks and duties.

There are many things I wanted to do while I was off for four months. I wanted to read the books I had been saving to read, see movies that I had put off seeing, visit friends that I had not seen for a while, and go to concerts. I also wanted to go to the theatre, play golf, participate in church functions, write a book, get a new job, and finally host the auction for the scholarship fund. (Wow, I am making myself tired just writing this). You see, we must make and set priorities at every of our lives because life is a continuum and it is infinite — not just a moment in time.

I had to prioritize the things I needed to accomplish in four months and continue to do the others in stride as I live and as I prepare to start another venture. The first priority was to get another job, followed by writing this book, and then getting the items and plans for the upcoming auction for my scholarship fund raiser. Even while off, you still need to prioritize. This is true on the weekend, while on vacation, or on your "goof-off" day. Get the people around you to help with the prioritization. Their involvement in the process will help when you are asking and expecting accountability from them.

Richard Carlson, author of *Don't Sweat The Small Stuff* said "Remind yourself that when you die, your in-basket won't be empty." Therefore, we must do the important things first, and then do the other activities in order and as time permits.

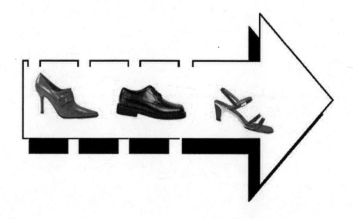

*"Nothing instills a sense of
power and confidence like
having done your homework.
Our battle cry must become,
'BE PREPARED.'*

*Be prepared,
know what you are
striving for; be prepared
with a plan A and B and even a plan
C and D; be prepared to surmount
obstacles that may be
placed in your way; be prepared
to pick yourself up and start
over again if you should stumble
and fall; be prepared to BE
the BEST."*

Karen "Penny" Kerr
Principal
Chicago Public Schools
Chicago, Illinois

48

Do Your Work First

When we were in the mist of a merger and acquisition a lot of things ended upon my desk. People wanted me to be in meetings and part of various teams. Now it is good to be wanted, but I had my work to do so I graciously thanked them for thinking of me. On several occasions I suggested they use someone else to help on their teams and I would serve as a consultant or sponsor of the teams.

On one occasion when we were into one of the many transitions and needed to hire new managers, the members of the management team wanted my input on perspective candidates. I asked my first-line managers to do the first round of interviewing and I promise to give my opinion in the final round. This technique served two purposes: first it gave the managers the experience of interviewing and building confidence in themselves and their teammates. Secondly, it gave me some time for my work.

Once we were putting together a team for a project and my manager asked me to be on the team. I convinced him to let someone else serve on the team as leader and I would serve as sponsor. This kept me in the loop without having to attend all the meetings. This also gave one of my employees a chance to get exposure and to gain experience. You can be at the center of the event, meeting or project without being in the center.

In doing your work, first determine what is important to your manager. On one occasion, my manager and I were in direct conflict as to what was important. I thought seeing the customers was important, especially during a time of change, mergers and acquisitions when customers are experiencing levels of uncertainty. My manager thought it was more important to stay in the office, read e-mails and check voice mails. While I disagreed with my manager, I did what was important to him.

Doing your work first is quite similar to the instructions you get when you are flying on an airplane. The flight attendants tell you, in the event oxygen is needed, put your oxygen mask on before assisting others.

In business and your organizations, do your work first, then you help others. This does not mean you are selfish but sometimes, it is a matter of survival. Without your oxygen, you will not be able physically or mentally to assist others, regardless of how much you may want to help.

A friend of mine often says, "I must do what I need to do, so I can do what I want to do." Doing your work first helps reduce the stress and anxiety.

"It is time for every one of us to roll up our sleeves and put ourselves at the top of our commitment list."
-Marian Wright Edelman

"Before healing others, heal thyself."
-Wolof proverb

"In life, all we have is our word and our reputation. Guard this closely by not letting enthusiasm cloud your responses. Ask when a customer needs something as opposed to automatically saying that I will get you that this afternoon. Maybe that can happen if all the moon and stars line up, but often, something goes wrong, especially if you rely on others for your response. And when you make that REALISTIC promise, DELIVER it."

J.T. Bailey
Executive Director
Redistributors of America
New Orleans, LA

Under Promise and Over Deliver

Please, please, do not over commit. People remember more about what you do than what you say you were going to do. I know a person who is always the first person to RSVP to invitations but she never shows up for events. She also never calls or gives a reason for not being present. She acts as if the situation never existed. It has become a game with some people in the group. They make sure she gets an invitation, and take bets that she will not show up and will fail to offer a reason why she missed the event.

There are those who commit to something and conveniently forget they made the commitment. You know if you have made a commitment or have given your word to perform. If you cannot fulfill your commitment, let the other person know about the changes in a timely manner. You can e-mail, phone, fax, or send a note by Morse code before the event, if you know you will be a "no show."

Do not over commit. There is just so much you will be able to do in a twenty-four hour period. There are people who get involved with several organizations, initiatives, causes or events. Sometimes they get on a lot of committees in their organizations. They are not effective on any of the committees or teams. Now, if their purpose is to have their names listed then they are effective, but if they want to be able to add substance to the groups, then they need time to plan. You cannot be effective if you spread yourself too thin.

For every initiative I am involved in, I use a barometer to help me determine the amount of time I will have available to fulfill my commitment. I need time to plan before the meeting. The nature of the function and the responsibility will determine how much time is needed behind the scene to prepare for the camera. It is better to under commit and over deliver. If you know that a project or request will take you five days to complete, then give a commitment to get back to the individuals in seven days. If you are able to deliver in five days or sooner, then you will be remembered as efficient as opposed to promising to deliver in five days and it takes you seven or more days to complete the task.

Allow more time for unforeseen events. If you think you can get to a location in twenty minutes then allow forty-five minutes for those obstacles that may occur. If you get to an event early, use the extra time to collect your thoughts. If arriving at an event early causes you stress because you dislike having unproductive downtime, then bring something with you to occupy your time. While you are waiting, you can read a book, respond to e-mails, write notes, or return phone calls.

If you say you will call at 9:00 am, then call at 9:00 am. If you say you will give a response on a certain date, then get back to the person on that date. Your customer, or the person waiting for the results would appreciate an update. Even if you do not have all of the answers you can at least give your audience a status and progress report. People will forgive you if you do not have all of the answers, but they will not forgive or forget that you did not live up to your promise. Communicate! Communicate! Communicate!

Just as in business, you have an obligation to your family and friends to live up to your commitments. Say what you will do and do what you say. Walk the walk and talk the talk. A friend's mother has a saying that I think is appropriate for this section. When she encounters one of her relatives who often does not honor what he said he was going to do, her saying is "If George wasn't a man of his word, he should have said so."

*"Delegation is a great
way to help others develop
new skills. It is also a great
way to help you develop as
a leader and as a mentor."*

Dale Tepp
Director of Human Resources
COLOR-BOX, Inc.
Atlanta, GA

Delegate

A good leader knows he or she cannot do it all, nor does the leader have the talent to do it all. Let other people help you and learn to use available resources. Ask for help. It is amazing—many people will help and assist you if you only ask. When you delegate, do not micromanage the process. Give credit and critique when the job or task is completed. Gail Evans, author of *Play Like A Man, Win Like A Woman* says, "Many women fail because they can't accept help." When I take on a project, I never question how I will accomplish it. Rather, I ask, "Who are the people I need on my team to help me accomplish this?"

Women make time for their families, their children, their church, and their community, but they do not know how to ask for help. Many women view asking for help as a sign of weakness. Others fear being perceived as being weak and some even doubt their own skills. It is healthy when you ask for help. People want to help you, so let them.

"Hire the best people, then delegate."
-Carol A. Taber

*"Networking without a
Relationship Development
Goal is an exercise in
futility."*

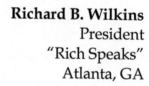

Richard B. Wilkins
President
"Rich Speaks"
Atlanta, GA

Network

Keep in touch with people who can make a difference. I do this via phone calls, e-mails, notes, and holiday correspondence. I have a very current address book, both electronic and hard copy which helps me stay in touch. There are very few major cities in America where I do not know someone. When I need information, someone to chat with and spend time with during long layovers or during visits to those areas, I always have someone I can call. Business cards, addresses and e-mail addresses should not be used just to fill your rolodex or electronic data file, but should be used as tools to effectively cultivate and build customer service networks.

Keep in touch, not because you may need a person, but rather because they may need you. This will give you a chance to showcase your abilities and help propel your own agenda. Seek a relentless person not a busy person. You never know when you will need a favor. You never know when someone will need your skills and expertise. This could be your golden opportunity. Sometimes, it can be monetarily rewarding and other times, it can be just the exposure you need.

I have relocated around the country a few times. Each time I relocated, people would ask me if I knew anyone in the city to which I was relocating. Usually, the answer was "No, but I am sure I will soon." In every city and town, there is usually a person who knows someone in that city and that person knows someone, and that person knows someone… and so it goes.

Network outside of the work environment such as in your church, social organizations, civic organizations, political arenas, and children career programs. In networking, the trick is learning to make the "net" work by identifying people you want and need to associate with. Set up specific times to be with them. Do not let the saying "Let's get together sometime" be a trademark of habit in expression where you do nothing. "Let's get together" is usually a sure way for nothing to happen. Take out your day planner, set a date and a game plan.

If you concentrate, spend time and get to know at least one new person per month that equals 12 persons per year. If each of these twelve persons introduces you to one other person, your "new person chain" has grown to 24 persons.

My annual goal is to get to know at least one new person each month by planning a specific time to get to know them. We may do lunch, play tennis, golf, attend sporting or cultural events, go shopping, or take day trips. Whatever the interest, the key is to make it happen now, not someday. Focus on each individual person and get to know as much about as possible about him or her.

I try to get to know people in various fields of expertise. It does not add a lot of value if all of your friends, associates, and acquaintances think and have the same skills as you. Get to know people in accounting, legal, investments, ministry, schools, universities, landscaping, plumbing, etc. These same people also need to know what you bring to the party. They need to know your skills, desires, visions and goals. You never know who can help you or where you can assist others. If you are uncomfortable networking one on one, then do your networking in pairs or groups. Two or more people can meet others for lunch, tennis, golf, shopping, movie, etc. This will help each person to get to know more people in a more comfortable setting.

Keep in touch because everyone is so mobile and you never know where people will turn up. One of my representatives was having a difficult time getting to see a target client. During one of our conversations she mentioned her frustration at not being able to get an appointment. I asked her who was the president at that company. After she gave me the name and phone number, I phoned him. We were able to get in to see this target client in a matter of weeks. The president was a sales representative for a customer when I had been a manufacturer's representative calling on the same customer many years prior. Therefore, it was easier to get in to see him because no introduction was necessary. It pays to keep in touch because the personal contacts can be valuable as you navigate through your career.

Let key people know what you are working on and share some of the key ideas you may have. Find a way to identify people who have done something similar to what you want to do. Engage them in dialogue. They may be able to help or at least direct you to others who can assist you. If you want to be a caterer, then you should talk to people who have started and are in the catering business. If you want to get your basement finished, then talk to someone who has done it or has had it done to get his or her feedback. If you want to start a business, then talk to someone who has started a business. By talking with the people who have done the thing you want to do, they will be able to shed some light on what works, as well as some of the pitfalls you may encounter.

When I was kicking around the idea of writing this book, I discussed my plan with my pastor, Rev. Walter Kimbrough, Senior Pastor of Cascade United Methodist Church in Atlanta. Pastor Kimbrough is a published author and contributor to several books such as, *"The Irresistible Urge To Preach"* and *"365 Meditations for Men."* I shared the concept with him. "You must write the book," he said. Another person I know told me about a publisher who may be willing to work with me on my book. I began to work with the publisher and waited patiently for the finished book. Unfortunately, the publisher began to give excuses as to why the book was delayed. It became clear that he was not going to deliver me a finished product. Hence, if I wanted this book published I had to find another alternative. I found a designer, printer, and others to assist me in getting this book published. Now here is the book and I thank you for reading it.

Do not be afraid to ask for help from people who are doing the kinds of things you want to do. I am not advocating that you talk to just anyone. You have to be careful where and with whom you share ideas. Communicate and converse with people who will give you valid, specific input and feedback.

The key to networking is to find, develop, discover, and cultivate your style to make the "net" work.

"You can make more friends in two months by becoming interested in other people than you can in two years by trying to get other people interested in you."
-Dale Carnegie

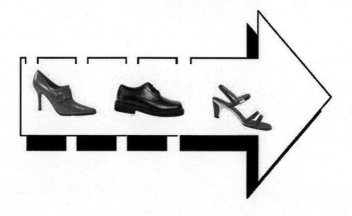

"Success becomes real when we dare to dream big and work as if everything depends on us. The ball has been placed in our hands and we must decide what we will do with it."

Rev. Walter L. Kimbrough
Senior Pastor
Cascade United Methodist Church
Atlanta, GA

Broaden Your Horizon

Get involved in the community. Attend seminars, classes, and events. Attend conferences on things you know little about. Embrace your curiosity.

Be open and inquire about learning different things. Having useful knowledge and the ability to converse about something your customer may have a passion for, or an interest in, will earn you respect. People like to do business with people who take an interest in the things they are interested in. Expanding your boundaries about new things will give you the opportunity to see how other groups operate. As you broaden your horizon, you develop new interests and invite comparison to the things you already know. If the opportunity or circumstance does not exist, then create it.

Laura Lowing, Director of Marketing at Network Services, saw a need for women in the paper and packaging industry to have a forum to connect, dialogue and strategize. As late as 2002, the organization did not exist. Laura and other women who were members of the Network Associates, Inc., a Marketing and Buying group, created an association - Women In Network (WIN). Laura got her president, Jim Alexy, and other key management personnel to support and sponsor this venture. Her manager was not a silent partner in the background. He endorsed the groups' mission, recognized its value in professional development and supported it by attending the initial meeting. He has committed financial support and other resources to the group. Laura invited other women who were suppliers, owners, and vendors to participate. Consequently, if the opportunity does not already exist, then create it.

Mission of Women In Network

Their mission is to provide women executives within the Network organization a forum in which ideas, information and experiences can be shared in a supportive environment.

In support of this mission, WIN will strive to enhance the status of women in the paper distribution business through the establishment of a close knit network. WIN will promote professional growth, mentoring and leadership among the membership and establish programs to facilitate personal development and career advancement.

In May 1989, *Restaurant Business*, a trade publication, convened a group of high-level women executives to sponsor the formation of a national organization committed to the career advancement of women throughout the foodservice and hospitality industries. This national organization became known as Women Foodservice Forum (WFF).

The Women's Foodservice Forum is the foodservice industry partner in promoting leadership development and career advancement of executive women for the benefit of the foodservice industry. The purpose of the WFF is to create an awareness of the status of women in the foodservice industry and the benefits of more diversified leadership. At the heart of the Women's Foodservice Forum is the shared dream of opening doors to leadership positions for more women.

The Mission of WFF is to engage the foodservice industry to develop leadership talent and ensure career advancement for executive women. The WFF Vision is to create an industry of choice with a leadership profile that mirrors society and our customers.

Some of the programs the WFF offer are: Annual Leadership Development Conference, WFF Mentor Executive and Emerging Leadership conference, Regional Connects which are regionalized network events, and Executive research that research benchmarks for the industry and address the issues of highest concern to the membership.

Gerry Fernandez saw a need for more minorities and diversity in management and ownership in the foodservice and hospitality industry. This type of forum did not exist in 1997, so Gerry convinced his manager at General Mills that this would be a good thing. Gerry, along with others, created the Multicultural Foodservice and Hospitality Alliance(MFHA). As I write this book, the membership is growing as key persons from Coca Cola, General Mills, McDonalds, Burger King, Brinker, and other major corporations, are working to make a difference in the professional development of workers at all levels in the foodservice and hospitality industry.

When you get to know people in other industries and in businesses other than the industry you are in, there will be opportunities to share, trade information and build coalitions to better serve and gain knowledge of the marketplace. If customers you are doing business with are having issues and problems, they are usually having the same or similar issues with other manufacturers.

Involvement in other arenas also helps you develop professionally. Broadening your horizon also means you are willing to stretch outside of your comfort zone and try something new and different. Who knows? You just might like your new surroundings, your new view and wonder what took you so long to try a new and different venture or approach.

A quick way to broaden your horizon is to get involved with activities in your community, join civic clubs, groups and organizations. Another way is to broaden your view is to travel, relocate, learn a new language or start a business. The possibilities are endless if you would just dare to take a step out of the comfort zone.

"Do not follow where the path may lead. Go instead where there is no path and leave a trail."
Anonymous

"A man's reach should exceed his grasp or what's a heaven for?"
-Shakespeare

"When one understands, respects and values the diversity of our work force, ultimately everyone wins in the creation of success and wealth."

Lucretia Payton-Stewart, PhD
President,
Lucretia Payton-Stewart & Associates
Professor, Georgia State University
Educational Policy Studies
Atlanta, GA

Promote Each Other

Praise the work of others when they do things for you or when they do a good job. Identify other women, minorities and people of color who you can bring along on the journey. Find ways you can promote for inclusion. Introduce them to facets of the organization, and involve them so they can be successful and progressive.

I get no special thrill or joy from being the only woman or person of color in a meeting or situation. It is up to the person who is in a position to make a change, to identify women and other people of color who you can help. If not us, then who? If not now, then when? If not here, then where? If not this, then what?

From 1999-2001, when I was at Georgia Pacific Tissue, more than 25% of Georgia Pacific Tissues' outside sales force, in our division, were women. It helped that we had in our department two females who were Directors of Sales. Beryl Kemp was Director of National Accounts and I was Director of National Chain Distribution. We were the first women director of sales at Georgia Pacific Tissue, and the year was 1999. The two of us went to great lengths to include rather than exclude. We wanted as many women, minorities and people of color to be in key positions. Some people are of the opinion that women and people of color do not want other women or other people of color to be at their level. This is not true. We recognize that when we succeed, all women succeed, and the more diversity involved in the process, the greater the results. Beryl knew a lot of people and I personally owe her a "thanks" for the method in which she included other women at Georgia Pacific in the process. Let me repeat, *If not us, then who… if not now, then when… If not here… then where?*

Let's not fall into the trap or use the excuse that if one minority or if one woman does not work out, then none will. Look at the world as it is. If one white male is not successful, he is usually replaced with another male. Management should be diligent in their quest to find, groom, mentor and promote qualified women. Women make up 51% of the United States population; African Americans represent 12.6%. Of the entire U.S. workforce of 140,863,000, 60% are women, and 12.5% are women of color. These numbers validate that there are others who we can seek, hire, and develop to be inclusive. We should seek to include a more diverse group of candidates without sacrificing or overlooking the other groups and genders.

Our job is not complete when we seek diversity. We must encourage each other to help ensure success, progression, and upward mobility. **Mentoring and Networking through the LandMinds** is paramount to success. Just as a nation would not send its Navy out to sea without the proper amount of ammunition and provisions for the journey, managers or representatives should not send their people out untrained. To ill prepare your employees is tantamount to setting your people or yourself up for failure. If we fail to mentor and nurture the people we hire, our conviction for inclusion is neither real nor sincere.

"There is no limit to what a woman (man) can do or where she (he) can go if she (he) doesn't mind who gets the credit."
-Robert W. Woodruff

"A sure way for one to lift himself up is by helping to lift someone else."
-Booker T. Washington

*"You must be guided by your
own principles and convictions."*

Jacqueline C. Gholson
District School Social Worker
Shaker Heights City School District
Shaker Heights, OH

Be True to Your Convictions

When you are in a position to make a difference and do not do it, then shame on you. If you are filling positions or promoting, insist upon a variety from which to choose.

Truett Cathy is someone whom I admire when it comes to being true to one's beliefs and conviction. Mr. Cathy is the Founder and CEO of Chick-Fil-A, one of the premier Quick-Service Restaurants Chains. I had the pleasure of meeting Mr. Cathy in 1989 when I was calling on Chick-Fil-A Corporation. His restaurants are not open on Sundays because he believes this day is for family and worship time. He told me that people have advised him as to how much money he loses because the restaurants are not open on Sundays. He said, "And I will continue to lose money if that is the case because they will not be open on Sundays." Here is a person who believes in family times and is willing to forgo more money for his beliefs. Even in changing times, when other restaurants and establishments are open for business on Sundays, all of Chick-Fil-A restaurants are closed. By all means, be true to your convictions.

In the mid nineties, during one of our transi - tions, we had a meeting to rationalize our sales force in relation to other departments in the company and industry. We were analyzing each sales person using such criteria as number of years in the industry, size of territory, skill sets needed, etc.

At the conclusion of our analysis, each sales person was assigned a grade level which determined his or her salary range. With this task completed, we were ready to continue with the next phase, but before we could move on, several people said, "I now need for this person or that person to have a different compensation package." I took a stand and said that I cannot support exceptions without real facts or just because the person has the right name. I then asked the question, "If we removed the person's name how would they fit in the equation?" Most said, "You cannot do analysis with the names removed." I stated that the equation should work and be fair regardless of whose name is being used. If the guidelines we had just established were good enough for the masses, then it had to be good enough for the special interest groups.

I have a difficult time supporting special exceptions without real facts. I am pleased to say that several people in the room also supported me, and we were able to be objective. Be true to your convictions.

It is amazing how women and men look at situations and have different opinions based upon gender. One day when we were in a meeting, a woman who had recently had a baby left early that day due to family needs. Several men and women in the room immediately remarked, "She has a family, so why is she working?" The reason why this reaction stood out so clearly to me is earlier in the day I heard different comments when a man in the same department took off early because his son was getting braces. I heard those same men and women responded to his situation by saying, "Isn't he a good father to want to be with his son when he gets his braces?"

Similar responses are voiced when men get custody of children. Isn't he wonderful for getting custody of the children? In separations and divorces, women get the children 80% of the time and rarely does anyone compliment them on the job they do as a single parent. Women perform as single parents and they often have lower income than men, and get or receive much less support from families and friends.

Being true to your convictions can be humorous also. During the early 80's, a girlfriend and I went shopping for shoes. On the drive back from the shoe store, we stopped at a service station to get a soda from the machine outside of the building. As I walked back to the car without a soda, my friend asked me "What's wrong? Was the machine broken?" I said, "No, I am not going to pay that price for a soda." She replied, "You have more than $400.00 worth of shoes in the trunk of the car but you won't pay seventy-five cents for a soda?" "Yes, that's right, I am not going to pay that price for the soda, it's the principle of the matter," I said. At the next station, I was able to purchase a soda for fifty cents. "I am glad you found one in your price range, because if not, I was going give you the money for the soda," my friend said.

I was being true to my convictions because people who know me know I never met a pair of shoes that I did not like. And as for the soda, well, I could do without it.

"To thy own self be true."
-William Shakespeare

Choose Your Shoes…Then Take a Walk

"No matter what position you hold in an organization, visibility and availability are key to your success. Take part of every day to talk to your boss, your peers, your subordinates to, ensure you have identified problems and kept others informed of important decisions."

Dale Tepp
Director of Human Resources
COLOR-BOX, Inc.
Atlanta, GA

Be Visible

You must get involved to get noticed. Try to get a role on a team or responsibility on a key project. Introduce yourself to key people and do not wait for them to come to you or to seek you out. Be reminded that if you are able to get key roles and projects, there are drawbacks if you do not produce or perform well. But, like the adage, nothing ventured, nothing gained; so go for it.

Most people go into ventures with the thought that they will be successful. They do not allow failure to be an option. Even if the results are not as stellar as you would have liked, or hoped for, the experiences you gain will be valuable for the next venture. Allow that experience to become part of your playbook.

If you are a member of organizations, work on a committee or a team. Notice, I said work, and that means not just putting your name on the committee or team list. Remember not to get on too many committees because "more and many" in this case, are not better. It is easier for people to get to know who you are and what you can do if you are involved and not just a bench member.

Another way to help your visibility is to develop your signature saying. This can be a response to a simple, common question. Example: When someone speaks and asks "How are you"? Most people respond by saying *Fine*. I say, *fabulous*, or *marvelous, but you know that already*. Usually, their response is "Yes, I knew that." Again, my response causes them to take notice. Be different; have a sense of humor and just go with it.

My minister's favorite response is *fantastically well*. Another person I know responds by saying, *if I got any better I would be perfect*, another says, *fine as frog's hair*, and yet another says, *just short of phenomenal*.

When I say, *"help me understand,"* I am questioning for clarity and I want to get the person to think logically as they follow the process. I know another woman who often says, *"are you kidding?"* to express her disbelief or she will say *"nice try, but no,"* when she is trying to get her people to make logical decisions. Another woman friend often says, *"are you crazy?"* And, she can carry it off. Most people who know her expect it when she is expressing disbelief. A man I know often uses, *"how do you eat an elephant?"* He is trying to make a point that the job or task may appear monumental but the goal can be accomplished if it is tackled one point at a time.

Develop your signature saying to be set apart.

"Let your light so shine that they may see your good works."
-Matthew 5:16.

"You've got to find a way to let people know you're there."
-Nikki Giovanni

*"Success in business and
personal life comes from
being flexible. Be willing
to make the necessary
changes in your vision to
involve others."*

Cleretta Thomas Blackmon
Publisher/CEO
Mobile Beacon Newspaper
Mobile, AL

Be Flexible

Your way is not the only way to do something. You may find that when you allow others to offer suggestions or do a job differently, you might like it or you may be able to gather ideas as to how you can improve or adjust it.

When I was recuperating from surgery, my mother came to spend some time with me. My mother likes being busy so she did the laundry for me during her stay. I remember her coming down the stairs, saying, "I did the linen, but I am not sure if I folded the towels correctly." When I finally gained my composure I said, "Mom, you have me confused with one of your other daughters, because I do not care how you folded the towels. I just want to thank you for doing the laundry."

Some people need and expect to have things done a certain way. For something so trivial, I only cared that the laundry was clean and put away. I was not concerned how the towels were folded because they would be used soon enough and will have to be done all over again. Don't sweat the small stuff and be flexible.

Right after I hired a new assistant, she and I were designing a presentation. During the design phase, I noticed that she appeared nervous so I encouraged her to speak up. She had ideas on the presentation that were great, and of course, they enhanced the outcome of the presentation. I was flexible in my thought process and discovered the benefit of new, creative talent—a talent that confirmed my way was not the only way to get the job done. Be flexible.

"Leadership is the art of getting someone to do something you want done because he wants to do it."
-Dwight D. Eisenhower

Choose Your Shoes...Then Take a Walk

> *"Establishing a comfort level means having trust and it must be established on both sides of the equation. Always remember how hard it is to establish trust and how easy it is to lose trust."*

Bill Sweaney
Senior Director of Sales-US
SCA Tissue North America, LLC
Neenah, WI

Establish a Comfort Level

You should start out in any new position getting your employees comfortable with you. Get to know the spouses, partners, significant others of the people who will be reporting to you and include them in your dinners or other events and functions. This is especially important early into the working relationship which will give them the opportunity to get to know you. Significant others should know who their partner is working with, particularly if the partner is a male and the manager is female. They need time to meet you and become comfortable with you. Whether we want to believe it or not, getting people comfortable with you can mean a world of difference in their perception of you and the company.

Getting to know other important persons in your employees' family will also give you something else in common with the employee or manager which allows for additional bonding. It is good for children to know the manager. When you have to call the employee and the children answer the phone, you won't have to explain who you are or why you are calling. It is good for the children to also have an idea of the company and organization.

When you get to know your employees in their environment, you have the opportunity to see how they function with their spouses, significant others and their children. Most people remember the small things. Send little mementos for the birthdays, anniversaries or special occasions of your direct reports.

At one point in my career I inherited an office manager, and initially, she was a little apprehensive about working for me because we had never met. When some people heard that she would be working with me they immediately called her to try to gauge her feelings. "How will you feel working for an African American woman?" they asked. She said she was okay with it. I made a special trip to meet her and her husband. We had dinner and that weekend I spent time helping her with her flower garden because I had time on my hands, and I love flowers. She needed to develop a comfort level with me because this was a new venture for our company—a woman of color as a manager.

I reflected at the irony of the fact that people asked her how she would feel working for a woman of color, but I never recalled anyone asking, "How do you feel working for a white male?"

As I strive to establish a comfort level, I hope people will like me, but more importantly I strive for respect and integrity in all I do. At the end of the day, if I can look a person in the eyes and myself in the mirror and know I have been fair, to me, this has been a good day. Fair to me means imagining if I were placed in that situation and this was happening to me. Would it be fair and would I be pleased with the outcome?

"Tell me, I'll forget. Show me, I may remember. But involve me and I'll understand."
-Chinese Proverb

"Leadership by mandate is hollow, and results in shallow commitment. By involving people as owners of ideas, the vision becomes theirs, and the power of their idea multiplies."

Greg Linnemanstons
President
Weidert Group, Inc.
Appleton, WI

Involve People

Involve people in the situation or task, and they will be more accepting with the outcome and results. If you dictate to them how it should be, how it needs to be and how it must be, people will be less likely to receive it positively and enthusiastically. Involving people in the process is like playing to their egos and needs which usually makes people feel special.

When we relocated our office, the administrative assistants complained that there was a lot of extra work to do. I told them that I would hire a temp to help them. They needed to give to me in writing the tasks this person would perform; then, the three assistants and I would interview and hire the temp. Two weeks went by and I asked them when they were going to get the list to me. They said they would get it to me soon.

After six weeks, I told them that I must have missed the list because I had not seen it. They said, "Things have gotten better and we can handle the work load." Had I not listened, heard them and allowed them to find a solution they would have continued to complain. I involved them in the process, which was what they wanted and needed.

"Learn to communicate verbally, in writing, and through strong body language. Take every opportunity to speak to a group, write a report, etc. It gets easier and your skills will improve the more you do it."

Laura Ann Lowing
Secretary Women In Network (WIN)
Director of Marketing
Network Services Company
Mount Prospect, IL

Communicate

When issues and circumstances arise, direct the questions to the source. Communicate for understanding. Question for clarity and not for blame as you listen to understand and seek to be understood.

Women tend to destroy friendships because a person may have done something they did not like. Rather than confront the person and gain clarity, they discard the relationship. My style is to tell the person what they did and how it made me feel rather than destroy a friendship. If a person knows how his actions adversely affects you and a person chooses to change, then this is good. If the person chooses not to care, and continues to act the same way, then that's okay too. At least he or she knows how you feel. It is now up to you to decide how you will proceed with the relationship.

Communication is easy if we would just make the effort. I am often perplexed when people say they could not connect with others. Even ET phoned home. With all of the tools and means of communicating on this earth, surely we can inform others when plans and circumstances change. Err on the side of over communicating rather than under communicating.

"I am a firm believer that people come into your life for many reasons, one of them being to teach and let you learn. Besides friendship, Versie Black also taught and let me learn."

Beryl E. Kemp
Director of Sales
National Account
Georgia Pacific Corp.
Atlanta, GA

R-E-S-P-E-C-T

Treat others with respect. Regardless of their station in life, people are human, with feelings, and you should treat them with respect no matter where you find them. The young person working in the warehouse today, may be the president or owner tomorrow.

Earlier in my career, I made it a personal goal to know all employees of my customers regardless of their position within the company. This approach proved invaluable and served me well on numerous occasions. There were times when my truck would invariably be late for an appointment and the buyer needed the product yesterday. Sometimes a phone call to the warehouse manager would get me some much needed relief. He would help me to reschedule or fit my trucks into an unloading slot to accommodate the buyer. Other times, I may have needed a favor to have samples pulled and the guys in the warehouse would interrupt their work and pull samples for me.

There was a young man working in the warehouse when I started my career with this particular customer. Sixteen years later, he was the person at this same account who could make or break us. He was the person who decided which manufacturer would get the go ahead to be the main supplier. The company I worked for was able to maintain this account due, in part, to relationships I had developed and maintained through the years.

Accept people where they are. If you take time to get to know them, you will usually find something interesting and unique that sets them apart. This is what people and life are about. Sometimes what you discover is the outside what appearance can be drastically different from is on the inside. People won't remember what you say, but they will remember how you make them feel.

As you interact with people, try not to be too judgmental. What you see initially may not necessarily be the true picture. I was waiting in the lobby to see a potential client. An older man came in, sat down beside me and we engaged in a conversation. Had I judged him by his appearance alone on this particular day, I would have said he did not belong in the building. I am glad that I was friendly and kind to the stranger because as it turned out, the stranger was the owner of the company. I am glad my mother instilled and reinforced in all of her children early in life that you can't judge a book by its cover.

We should respect people regardless of their positions and station in life, and we should not hold grudges or burn bridges. The world is a small place and people are so mobile. You never know when or where you will see a person from your past. Holding grudges requires energy that is wasted because in the end, little is accomplished. If we are able to separate the event or situation from the person, it may help us let go of the issues that trouble us. Do not burn bridges because this is a small world. Mobility is the norm and you never know where people will be tomorrow.

Develop a style that reduces the likelihood of putting people on the defense or hurting their feelings. I try to use humor or ask thought-provoking questions to cause people to think. I recall a flight attendant using humor as we were landing at the Los Angeles airport after a long flight from Tokyo. When passengers began getting up and collecting their bags before the plane reached the gate, she calmly said, "Rarely in aviation history has a passenger reached the gate before the plane, so please keep your seats." The flight attendant could have said, "Please stay seated." However, she chose to use humor, which got more attention, evoked laughter and helped to diffuse the situation.

Rather than tell someone what they just said or did was a little less than logical, I say, "Help me understand." This gives us a chance to work through the situation and hopefully allow us to arrive at a solution. When my sales people called to explain a request from a customer, they often asked, "what should we do?" I would turn it around and together we would review the 5 W's. What do you want to do? Why do you want to do it? What do you want the outcome to be? If not this, then what do you want to offer as an alternative? Who has to know and who has the authority to make that decision?

Treating people with respect is paramount. What's more, it will be appreciated.

"Do not insult an alligator until you've crossed the river."
-African Proverb

Choose Your Shoes...Then Take a Walk

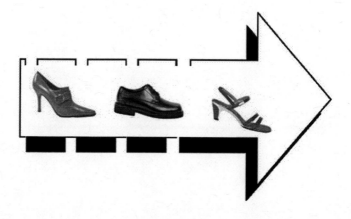

"Know your audience - they are the ones receiving your message. What will they accept? What will they reject? Unless you know, you may as well cast your words to the wind."

Sandra Ahern
Manager of Training & Development
J. M. Huber Corporation
Atlanta, GA

Know Your Audience

See your audience as it is and not as you think it should be. Try to use examples, ideas, and points of discussions that are applicable to them. Example: I have heard people ask the audience, "Where were you when John F. Kennedy or Martin Luther King, Jr. was killed?" Or they ask, "Where were you when Neil Armstrong walked on the moon?" These are good questions because most people can relate to where they were, what they were doing, what they were thinking and how they felt when these events happened. However, these events have no real meaning or at least, not the same effect if you are talking to audiences who were not born yet. I cannot relate to the emotions, feelings and reactions that my parent's generation felt when Pearl Harbor was bombed. Likewise, there are generations that cannot feel what my generation felt about the Kennedy and King assassinations.

Know your audience. When you are trying to reach people in the audience, use examples they can relate to and those that the generation can understand. I remember taking a skill development class and the instructor used music as an ice breaker. She played songs from the 50's and the 60's and asked the teams to name the songs for points. The teams failed miserably. I suggested that she use music from the 70's and the 80's the next day. I made this suggestion because I had observed that the audience and most of the students in the class were born in the 70's; therefore, the music from the 50's and 60's was ancient to them. The next day, the students got into the game, the competition heated up, and they had fun because the trivia was from their generation and they knew some of the answers.

Now, I am not advocating or suggesting history is unimportant. It is very important, but you must know what turns the audience on if you want participation.

Recently, I was talking with a friend and he told me his daughter (age 29) asked him to explain a metaphor he used when he was having a conversation with her. His daughter was sharing with him how much she respected a certain person's opinion about the job market and working situations. "I am not sure that this particular individual is the best qualified person to give you that advice, because he has never hit a lick at a snake," her father said. My friend was perplexed. He thought everyone including his daughter understood the metaphor meant the person giving the advice had not held a job and therefore would not be the best person to give a qualified opinion.

When we become more cognizant of our audience, we will find that for someone of a different generation, the metaphors must be applicable to that generation. We cannot assume everyone is on the same page and at the same level of understanding.

"When you know you are being tested, the key is not letting the "tester" know you realize it. Hold your ground and don't cave in."

Garth Hess
General Manager
C. A. Curtze Company
Erie, PA

Know When You Are Being Tested

Teach yourself to act and not to react. Do not let other people's monkey become your monkey. Sexual harassment was not in vogue or in the forefront when I started working in the business world in 1974. As a matter of fact, some people went to great lengths to make women uncomfortable in our work environment.

Each of us has a responsibility to make today's environment a pleasure for all to work, function and be successful, regardless of gender. Once we were at a major meeting with both women and men in the audience. During one of the presentations a comedian was part of the entertainment. His act consisted of some inappropriate remarks about women. In my opinion, his act really belonged in a nightclub and not in a sales environment of both sexes. I noticed that several of the women became uncomfortable. They looked at me in an attempt to gauge my reaction. Luckily, at this point in my career, I had developed a way not to let my facial expression be so easily read.

During the break, I spoke with the human resources person and he agreed with me that the presentation was out of line. However, when I had a conversation with my male counterparts, they said they did not see anything wrong with the comedian's act. " If your wife, daughter or mother was in the audience would the comedian's act still be appropriate?" I asked. They unanimously said, "No, it would not be appropriate." I responded to that statement by saying, "If it is not appropriate for your female family members, then it is not appropriate at this event because there are females in this audience." The important thing is not to react but to create action which makes a positive more lasting impact.

"The ultimate measure of a man is not where he stands in moment of comfort and convenience, but where he stands at times of challenge and controversy."
-Martin Luther King, Jr.

*"As women, we tend to
want to fight all the battles
and right all the wrongs,....
but as you will learn, you
can be much more influential
if you understand
which battle to fight, and
what that will accomplish
in the long run...."*

Beryl E. Kemp
Director of Sales
National Accounts
Georgia Pacific Corp.
Atlanta, GA

Pick Your Battles

You can't win them all. If you treat each and every issue as a cause to fight, you lose your effectiveness. Do not get so caught up in fighting each battle that you lose the war. When you choose to take on an issue, be prepared to see it through. Gather facts, rehearse your thoughts and eliminate emotions. Get others' input on the issue and particularly, get input from those whom you know are opposed to the issue. Be prepared not to be popular; be prepared for sabotage.

When there are issues that need to be resolved, do not whine. Enter the discussion with suggestions and thoughts of solutions, not with complaints that have neither merit nor substance. Your battles need and must have your true conviction. If you are in a whining mood, I suggest that you sell tickets and make it an event. Whining never accomplishes anything.

You want to win as we all do, but you should also recognize that neither you nor anyone wins all of the battles, all the time. You win some and the rest are delayed, canceled, rained out, or are a draw.

"Always hear what is not stated and understand the difference from the spoken word. Use of this rule will generate a truthful and accurate response."

Barbara A. McKinzie
Chief Financial Officer
Cook County Forest Preserve District
Chicago, IL

Listen to Hear

Do not participate in water cooler or hallway gossip. Confidential matters should stay confidential. When someone asks you, Do you know such and such? Are you aware that this is happening? Or, what is going on with various issues? They are really fishing for gossip or trivial information from you. Rather than giving your opinion and telling all you know, determine the reason for their interest and get them to share some of their insights. When you do not know everything about everything, usually people will volunteer information because they want to be the first to tell you a secret so you will think that they are privileged and "in the know". Therefore, listen and you will learn much.

Do not tell all that you know. Even if you know the answer, you should ask questions to engage people in dialogue from which you can gain information. You learn more from listening than you do by talking. You cannot hear if you are talking. I often refrain from talking about events and things I have done because I already know about those things. I have experienced them. I am more interested in hearing about others than I am in hearing myself talk. I particularly like groups where the dynamics change as the people come and go for various reasons. Listening and observing will prove to be a great learning arena as the landscape of people and personalities change.

When you "listen to hear," you gain a clearer understanding of other people's boundaries and parameters. As an example, one evening after dinner, an employee suggested that we have dessert. We were in agreement about the dessert. "There is a neat place right around the corner that has the best desserts," she said. We got in her car, got on the interstate and five miles later, we had not arrived at the restaurant. I turned to her and asked, "When do you think we will be there?" "Oh, in about 10 minutes," she said.

Apparently, this is a clear case where I should have listened to get a clearer understanding from this person as to the time and distance of the restaurant. My idea of 'right around the corner' is the ability to walk a few blocks, or at best, a mile. However, her idea within of 'right around the corner' was somewhere the same county! **Listen to Hear.**

Once I attended an event with another person. When we were ready to depart, we gave our thanks to the host and hostess. I turned around and the person I was with had begun another conversation that lasted fifteen minutes. Then he turned around and located someone else and got into another conversation that lasted 20-25 minutes. He could not understand when I said we have a different understanding of the phrase "we are leaving." To me, when we say "we are leaving," we should be out the door in a matter of minutes, not thirty-five minutes later. **Listen to Hear** to minimize confusion, misinterpretations and disappointments.

As you **Listen to Hear,** act as if everything you do will matter, because everything you do does matter. Depending on your position, you can make a statement or do something and instantly it is blown out of proportion. Others can do the same thing and it will be *boys being boys* or just business. Women have to play by different rules. What you do takes on a different life than if others did the same thing. Society has defined some of those rules and as women, we continue to build fences for ourselves. We need to remember that we can work within parameters while stretching the boundaries.

By listening you can determine a great deal from people as to their willingness to be helpful. As you actively listen, you can discern if a person is one who will offer you help. Which one do you think wants to be more helpful? The person who says, I will give you a life jacket; I am throwing you a lifeline, versus the one who says, I am going to throw you a grenade; here's a torpedo; or there's a missile coming at you? One set of phrases speaks of a desire to help an event be successful, or help a person to safe shores, while the second set of phrases denotes comments from a person who wants to derail, disrupt or alienate the person's ability to be successful. **Listen to Hear**.

Another good reason to **Listen to Hear** is you never know who knows who and the exact nature of their relationship. I was reminded of this recently. A girlfriend who lives 1200 miles away said to me on Monday evening, I understand you had brunch with so and so on yesterday (Sunday). I said, "Yes, and it was wonderful... but, how did you know?" She replied, the person you had brunch with is a friend of another woman who is the daughter of our friend, "Ms. X." Talk about a small world! You never know who is listening and what they are hearing.

Choose Your Shoes…Then Take a Walk

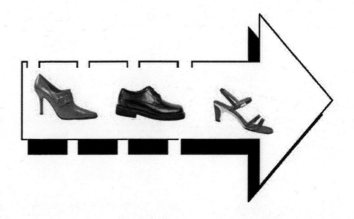

"Spend at least 10 minutes each day in silence to recharge. Problems will seem smaller, tasks less stressful and your mood much lighter."

Hortense D. Roberson
Media Specialist
Chicago Public Schools
Chicago, IL

Take Time to Recharge

Strive to be healthy and make it a habit to take care of yourself. We need to find time for ourselves. We must take inventory of ourselves because if we don't, we may end up bankrupt spiritually, physically, and emotionally. I often tell people to *Come in Out of the Rain*, rest and get the energy to continue the journey.

Sometimes we keep going even when our bodies are telling us we need to rest and take inventory of our health. Yet, if we get run down or really sick, we cannot function. Have a planned schedule to rest. My friends often tell me that I am working too hard. Yes, I work hard because I enjoy it and I play hard because I enjoy it. However, I rest hard and often because it is needed.

I know that this is the only body and mind I will ever have. Stress without rest changes my personality and I do not like my personality to be altered without my consent. I am able to keep going because I have planned relaxing time. I take a weekend every quarter to concentrate on me. It is important that I get my rest therefore I *Come in Out of The Rain* and get recharged.

The energizer bunny is a commercial and humans were not designed to be *Ever Ready*, always on the go and never winding down. Get real! You need to rest and get recharged. At the end of the day you are human with human mistakes, human errors, human frailties and human needs rest.

When you walk into your home, close out the outside world, it is time to spend time with your families and love ones. When you spend time with people who love you and are depending upon you, you need to be able to respond to them emotionally. If you have given it your gallant efforts, know that you gave it your best that day. You may have won a few, lost a few, but it is a good day if you win more than you lose. Again, at the end of the day you are human and need to recharge.

Women always have time to look after their families—children, spouse, parents, and other family members, but often feel guilty when they need time for themselves. Our health is important and I do not think it is selfish to be concerned about your health. If we don't take care of our health, the other aspects of family, children, events, and making a living won't be possible.

Take time for reflections. Everyday we do things that we consider ordinary. However, when we think, reflect, and determine the value of the relaxing experience, it can be invaluable. Reflections are valuable and should be an integral part of our daily operations.

Reflections serve as a stress reliever while also being an emotion filling station. Occasionally, we must pull in and be filled because no matter how hard we try to play and work, the emotion machine cannot run forever without refueling.

"I've talked to so many who believe they are supposed to be superhuman and bear up under all things. When they don't, they all too readily look for fault within themselves."
-Gloria Naylor

"I try to balance my life. When I'm home, I give quality time... I'm happy I've achieved what I have without losing my head."
-Patti LaBelle

"If management does not accept fun and laughter in the workplace, then the stress of the employees will result into a revolving door of personnel."

Joe Selzer
Vice President, Marketing & Sales
Wilkinson Manufacturing Company
Omaha, NE

Have Fun

I am not impressed with people who tell me they work all the time. I work hard and I play hard.

When you hear your manager's voice on the phone and you cringe, when you hate to get up in the morning to face a new day, when you lose the desire to win the fight, it is time to find something else to do. Regardless of what you do to earn a living (and most of us must work to survive), when it ceases to be fun, **Move On.**

In having fun, we should try to see the positive in situations and put things in perspective. I remember one winter, I was in Chicago and I was speaking via phone with a friend in Florida. I told him it was snowing and I was pleased to see the snow. "Snowing does not sound like a good thing to me," he said. I replied, "It is supposed to snow in Chicago in the winter. January without snow in Chicago is like July without sunshine in Florida. "Now that you put it that way, I agree," he said. Put things in perspective and you will be less stressed and more inclined to enjoy the ride.

"Life is to be lived. If you have to support yourself, you had bloody well better find some way that is going to be interesting."
-Katherine Hepburn

"If your business keeps you so busy you have no time for anything else, there must be something wrong either with you or with your business."
-Williams J.H. Boetecker

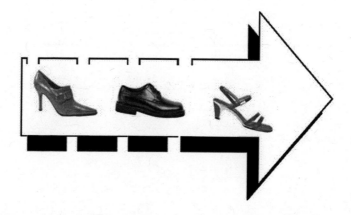

"Time is precious so use it wisely and with a purpose to move forward."

Marlene E. Earhart
Educator
Cincinnati Public Schools
Cincinnati, OH

Give Back

We have a responsibility, and I believe an obligation to give back to those people and institutions that have helped you or have had an influence on your life. Remember the people who were there for you and were influential in developing and shaping you into the person you have become. They include your parents, friends, family, relatives instructors, colleges, universities, churches, etc. I know people who have received a good education but will not contribute to their schools or alma mater. In fact, some default on loans after they complete their studies and have great jobs. The more you give, the more is given back to you.

"For unto whomsoever much is given, of him shall be much required."
Luke 12:48

Identify a cause that is important to you and find ways to support it. I served on the board of SafeHome—a shelter for domestically abused women and children. I was not good at answering the phones, but I knew sales people and other manufacturer's representatives.

I used my skills and contacts to get manufacturers to donate items to the shelter regularly. I also worked on the fund raising committee. Find your niche and you will be rewarded beyond your imagination. It will allow you to focus less on you and more on the big picture and the needs of others. There is something that we all can do. Someone helped you, and you have a responsibility to help others.

In 1999, I created the Versie M. Black Scholarship Fund to award scholarships to graduating seniors from my high school. I started it by making personal donations each year. Some of my friends heard about the scholarship fund and they began to send donations to it. With my friends contributing and helping to raise money for the students of J. F. Shields High School in Beatrice, Alabama, this has turned into an annual event.

Do not think for a moment that everyone wanted the venture to be a success. I continue the efforts because I refuse to let others derail my dream. I have been blessed and I want to give back to help others. Giving back shows what one person can do if she or he has a mind and desire to try.

"From what we get, we can make a living; from what we give, however, makes a life."
-Arthur Ashe

"Life's most urgent question is, "What are you doing for others?"
-Martin Luther King, Jr.

"Invest in human soul. Who knows, it might be a diamond in the rough."
- Mary McLeod Bethune

*"Humor reduces stress
and tension. There is
always a lighter side to
each situation and
humor helps to put
things in perspective."*

Naomi B. Harris
General Business Manager
Department of Justice
Federal Bureau of Prisons
Oakdale, LA

Have a Sense of Humor

Don't take yourself too seriously. One of the best ways to set your self apart is to be able to laugh at funny situations. I was on a flight from Salt Lake City, UT to Atlanta, GA right after the events of September 11, 2001. The flight attendant was trying to get everyone to listen to the safety instructions. He used humor by saying, "Once airborne, our flying time will be 196 minutes," instead of saying the flight will be arriving in Atlanta in three hours and sixteen minutes.

I immediately saw people stop and listen as they were calculating the time. "There are exit doors on this plane…somewhere," he said. Most flight attendants would have said there are four doors — one in the front, one in the rear, and one on each side. Most passengers would have expected these routine instructions and would not have paid much attention to the safety instructions. But when this attendant said, "there are exit doors somewhere" and he paused before elaborating, I saw people look around for the exit doors. Have a sense of humor and state the issues differently from the ordinary and the expected. It causes people to think and to remember.

When I check into a hotel the agent usually asks, "How many keys do you want?" To which my response is "One, unless you can find someone for me to give the other one to." I remember checking into the same hotel twice in three weeks. The same clerk checked me in both times. On my second check-in she asked me " How many keys do you want." I started to say, "one unless you can..." but she finished it for me and laughed. "Welcome back," she said.

When people ask me my name I say, "Versie Black." They often say, "That is a unique name, how do you spell it?" I respond "B-L-A-C-K." This often causes the person to smile and relax. Now I know they were asking me how to spell, "Versie" but when I spell "Black" which most people know how to spell, they remember.

When you need to buy time, using humor can help you gain time to gather your thoughts. Develop your own humorous style. I have a good friend who is retired. When anyone asks him what is he doing with his time now that he is retired? "Nothing and I do not start that until 11am," he replies.

Humor helps to reduce stress. I recall my manager and I had just finished seeing an important client and the negotiations had not gone as well as we had planned. To handle our disappointment, we laughed on the way home and gave different scenarios as to what we would say to our managers and the leaders of the company, if by some chance we lost the account. We did not intend to lose it but we needed to laugh to reduce the stress of what could have been. I am pleased to report that we kept the account but this was one time when laughter was the best medicine. We were able to regrouped to go the next round.

We need to be able to laugh at ourselves. My girlfriend Beryl and I were in Beijing and she was doing some serious negotiating with a person in the fashion district. Just to give you some information, negotiating is part of what Beryl has to do in her job so she feels that everything is negotiable. She is working the negotiation angle until I quietly tell her to give it up because the difference in what she is requesting amounts to $1.20. She turns to me and asks, "That's ALL!" I say, "Yeah." Now the table turns because less than twenty minutes later I find myself doing the same thing without thinking. She reminds me to pay the woman because it's less than $2.00. Needless to say, this set the tone for our trip and even today when we find ourselves getting really serious with issues and life, one or the other would say **Yuan** to remind us to relax, have a sense of humor and move on.

*"Corporate America is not
an environment for "loaners."
Team players and excellent
performers usually become and
gain mentors who provide
support."*

Cynthia Carter
Marketing Operations Manager
Xerox Corporation
Atlanta, GA

Develop a Support Group

Everyone needs a group of people from which he or she can get feedback. This is not a group of "yes" people but persons who will tell you what and how it is - not to hurt, but to help. Surround yourself with people who will be honest with you. Those people who will tell you the truth. They will tell you when you are stressing, when you need a break, when your idea is not so good, and when you are not yourself. Be sure your supporters are more than "yes" people. If you are not sure if they will tell you the truth, test them. Encourage honesty in your support group.

People in your support group should be people who are different from you. I already know what and how I think, therefore I need people in my support group who think and have opposite views from mine. According to Myers-Briggs' Type Indicator (MBTI), if your style is one of a "T-Thinker," then find a "F-Feeler." If you are a "S-Sensor," then find a "N-Intuitive." If you are a "J-Judging," then you need a "P- Perceive." If you are an "E-Extrovert," then you need an "I-Introvert" for your group. Likewise, if you review *Birkman's First Look* and if your management style is one of an Expediter or Communicator, then try to include people whose styles are Planner or Administrator.

The purpose for having different types of people in your group is to help keep you in tune to the real world and remind you that there are lots of opinions, thought processes and ideas that can help us grow and develop.

"Be thankful not only that you are an individual but also that others are different. The world needs all kinds, but it also needs to respect and use that individuality."
-Donald A. Laird

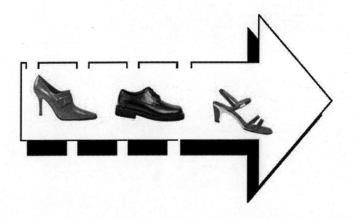

*"Life is changing and fleeting,
Happiness is not guaranteed."*

Jimmie L. Roberson
Cook County Sheriff's Dept.
Chicago, IL

Accept Change

We should learn to view changes as we do each New Year day—the opportunity to start fresh. Let's try to view change as seeing the positive: new surroundings, new people, and the opportunity to expand new horizons. We should be the change we want to see, because if not us, then who?

We can either accept change or create change but we cannot prevent it or control change. We can however, control how we react to change.

A friend of mine shared a situation where he knew it was time for him to change careers. He said when a new team joined the company, he knew he was not going to be part of the future company. It was evident as he was somehow often omitted from memos, forgotten to be copied on emails, and not informed of major meetings. He said his exit was a good thing because he knew he would have to find another career the day the management changed; therefore, he began to prepare himself to not be part of the team. Rather than dread the day he would be told that he would no longer be part of the team, he looked forward to leaving. He went on to say he was disappointed that it took thirteen months for them to complete this transition. In his opinion, management should have terminated him sooner.

When there are transitions, the morale of the personnel will be low. Everyone will be anticipating change and they will not be functioning to their full capacity. It is human nature to wait and see during times of transitions. Every work place, social organization, political arena, or family changes from time to time. We must learn to prepare for these changing times.

In this day and time, many companies will merge, acquire, or be acquired. You must have a game plan. It is best that you plan so others will not be in charge of your life. Some of the questions you must ask yourself are:

* If I survive the new structure and the new company, what do I want to do and what must I do to survive?

* If I am one who is chosen to be let go, what do I want to do now and what must I do for future employment?

This gets back to having a game plan for several scenarios. We should review these scenarios at various stages of our career and lives. We should not wait for a major change with our employer, our families, or organizations before we are thrust into having to make decisions and choices.

Sometimes you just have to go with it. You cannot wait for all the "T's" to be crossed or all of the "I's" to be dotted before you make a decision about possibilities of changes.

When there is a major change in your life, you should inform your family and friends right away. It is best that they hear it from you and not via the rumor mill or from others. When you personally inform people in your circle who need to know, they have the information first hand from you. Also if your family and friends hear information from others and not from you, they may be too embarrassed or hesitant about approaching you. Inform key people of any major change you may be experiencing so there are no surprises. Those who need to be informed include people in your community, church, committees, affiliations, associations, and organizations. This is also applicable in business as well as in our personal lives—marriages, divorces, promotions, and issues with families and children, etc.—so people will know how to react to situations and circumstances and not feel a sense of embarrassment. Prepare people to help them feel comfortable in knowing how to react or respond to the situation.

Deal with the change. Allow yourself to go through the process. The emotions are real, and pretending that the emotions do not exist will not make the situation less real or less of a reality. Handle it now. If you ignore the change or give it more time, this will not necessarily make the change go away. Try viewing each change and stage of change as an opportunity rather than something that is lost. Seek outside assistance to help you handle situations you do not have the talents, skills, or know how to answer. Get on with it.

When you make a decision regarding change or an event, move on. Revisiting and second-guessing the decision does not help the situation. This does not mean that the next time a similar situation occurs you will handle it the same way. Live and learn.

When others make mistakes or make a decision that you disagree with, do not keep reminding people of past errors. They know better than you do as to the mistakes and errors they have made in the past. Get on with it. It is what it is.

Move forward when there are personal set backs, family misunderstandings, business or career disappointments. Family members go for years without speaking to one another because someone did something to them years ago. At some point, one of the persons has to take the lead and clear up the misunderstanding. It seems such a shame to let an opportunity to enjoy family members and friends be wasted or lost because we cannot forgive one another and get on with it. Move on!

Change is the only constant and it is what it is. I believe that all people have the resilience to bounce back from situations. We all bounce back differently. How we bounce back has much to do with our experiences, our comfort level, our confidence, our outlook on life, and our faith. Opportunity is where prepared meets readiness, so we must prepare to bounce back as we prepare for change.

Some people go through a lifetime and never appreciate the opportunity to have a creative start because they want everything to remain the same.

"If you don't like the way the world is, you change it. You have an obligation to change it. You just do it one step at a time."
-Marian Wright Edelman

"You cannot relive or reshape the past. You can only learn from your experiences and move forward."

Linda Marie White
National President
Alpha Kappa Alpha Sorority, Inc.
Chicago, IL

Look Forward

The path has already been paved and there is little to be gained by constantly living in the past. When it is time, let it go. If you continue to dwell on how it used to be, you will miss how it is and will have little time to plan how it should be.

During one of the mergers, some people who had worked for one of the companies before the merger wanted to work for the new company. They kept saying, "I am back." I corrected them by explaining you cannot be back because this company is only six months old and you never worked here before. They had to learn to let go of the old. When you are faced with change, you need to take with you parts of the past for comfort and parts of the past for continuity.

The past experiences can serve as the backbone of an organization, but it cannot and must not be the mind of the future. Those who live in the past are doomed to be stagnant and realize little or no progress in the future. Look up to see the blessings on the pathway of success. Spend less time on what went wrong and focus more on the prize and what can be.

We need to move forward because we owe it to those who started the process. Granted, if you are just getting started on the road to your career, you could not have been a part of the past challenges. However, we all have a responsibility to continue the journey.

Women, people of color, white males, all of us have a chance to lengthen the path and continue on the road to diversity, inclusion, and success as we identify, recruit, mentor, and nurture those that come after us.

"Historic continuity with the past is not a duty, it is only a necessity."
-Oliver Wendell Holmes

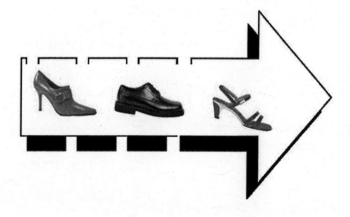

"Everyday our choices create more or... create less options for our own success."

Joanne Shufelt
Vice President, Sales
North American Commercial Business
Georgia-Pacific Corporation
Atlanta, GA

You Have Choices

Never forget as you look to the future, you have choices. Choices can dictate your future, but recognize and know choices have consequences. All choices have risks, and not all choices are easy.

There are no decisions that you make today that you cannot change tomorrow. You may not have the same options tomorrow as you do today but you can change a decision. You may have to choose different avenues or alternative paths. Accept no shortcomings. Accept nothing less than what you deserve. You need to have a realistic view of what is deserved. Get input from people who can and will give you clear guidance. If you can dream it, you can achieve it.

Know your walk-away-point. Always set parameters for yourself and know when you have had enough. Know when it is time. To do this you must be prepared and take inventory to enable yourself to be ready.

A few years back, Hewlett Packard had an ad that said "What If?" We should all ask ourselves the "What If" questions. What if there is a merger, acquisition, or a down size and if I am not chosen to be part of the company and the team? What will I do? What do I want to do? What will it take for me to do it? Then we should proceed with these parameters and criteria as we prepare ourselves. Once we establish our walk away point, the journey will be less frightening.

In everyday life we need to negotiate. When you are preparing to negotiate, know that you have choices and you need to be clear as to what you will accept. Also know when to say "No." Being prepared helps reduce the stress meter because you will have already determined when it will be time to walk away from the table and let someone else have it or start the process again.

"How one lives is, after all, one of the rights left to the individual when and if he has opportunity to choose."
-Alice Walker

Let things be done timely and in order.
-1 Corinthians 14:40

"Having fun is wealth and wealth is good health, family and friends. Good health includes mental, spiritual and physical health."

Darrell C. Claytor, CFP
Branch Manager
Securities America, Inc.
Shaker Heights, OH

Are We Having Fun Yet? (Still)?

When a job stops being fun and begins to just be "just a job," then it is time to move on. I would often ask my employees, "Are you having fun?" I also ask myself if I am still having fun. If the answer is yes and I am still feeling good, then I continue. When I have to struggle with an honest yes, it is time to re-evaluate the situation and the surroundings.

I do not mean that when you have a bad day it is time to evaluate; but when the thrill, the excitement, the desire to get up every day with a win-win attitude, then it is time to do something about the situation. You need to know when it is time to move on.

Make memories — most situations are not events unto themselves. I often say to my daughter, Valerie – "Let's make memories" as opposed to saying "Let's go to the mall, see a movie, visit the library, take in a ballgame, etc." Events are for the moment, while memories are for a lifetime.

"Life is not a problem to be solved, but a gift to be enjoyed."
- Anonymous

"There's really no such thing as an overnight success in business. Most successful business people have some extraordinary failures on their resumes', and success was born from their desire to overcome setbacks."

Greg Linnemanstons
President
Weidert Group, Inc.
Appleton, WI

If it Were Easy...

Anyone can do an easy job or task. The old adage, "Walk a mile in my shoes" translates to walk through business in your own shoes, but you must know which pair is appropriate for the occasion and the event.

You must learn when it is time for new shoes or when the old pair will suffice. You must pay attention to the signs and take off your shoes and rest. There are shoes for all seasons, for changing weather, terrain and circumstances.

The world is here for all of us including women and people of color to walk, but only we can decide when to take the first step. Only we can determine which direction the second step should be, and only we can determine the height of the third step. Only we can determine with whom to take step number four. We are in charge as to when other steps along the way will occur.

Although "Choose Your Shoes" is a book on tips for empowerment in the business world, the subjects that Versie highlights are applicable for everyday living. I recommend that every college student read this book to help gain insight into what it will take to be successful in today's world. So many of our young people think that if they have a good knowledge of technology then the other aspects of communication are secondary.

"Choose Your Shoes" is a winner.

Charles D. Gregg
Past President
University of Maryland Eastern Shore
National Alumni Association
Silver Spring, MD

Conclusion

Now that you have taken a journey with me, do not think it was easy. I developed a thicker skin along the way. I refused to let others derail my goals, deter my aspirations or prevent me from earning a living.

Some of these insights are humorous, but I want to remind you there were times when I was perplexed, hurt, angry, disappointed and confused. There were also times of great joy, fun, good humor, success and the opportunity to build lasting relationships. Emotions fueled my desire and determination to make it work for me. **When I Dream, I Dream in Color.**

I have had some great mentors in my business career. For each person who has played a part in my success, for each person who has given me support, for every individual who was there when I needed you, I say, "thank you." Equally, during my lifetime I have had some terrific influences from great people who helped to nurture my development. "Thank you" seems too little for all the genuine courtesy, professional counsel and friendship displayed during my evolution to greater rewards, personally and professionally. **I THANK YOU.**

This is not a blueprint for success. This is a process, not an event or program. It is my style, and it has worked for me. It may not be your style. Do not walk a mile in my shoes, rather develop your own style. Be comfortable with it and above all else, you can take steps if you want to change. Remember—just because you choose a pair of shoes and for some reason they stop fitting correctly, you do not have to continue to wear them.

You can always change the shoes you have chosen; you can buy another pair, change the height of the heel, the texture, the design or you can wear none at all. Life is a constant change and only you have the ingredients to make a great change.

As you walk through business and life in your shoes, learn which type of shoes are appropriate for the occasion and the event. Remember, it is never too late to redesign, make changes or take a walk.

About the Author

In her new book, *Choose Your Shoes... Then Take a Walk*, Versie M. Black, a career sales and marketing professional, shares insight into the abounding spirit that has given her a passion for accomplishment. You will find that her personal commitment, courage, and a never-say-die attitude expressed in this book will inspire you to reach beyond your limits with easy-to-adapt, workable guidelines.

Versie has developed others to points of success in business as a past Vice President of Sales at SCA Tissue (the first woman and first person of color), former Director of Sales for Georgia Pacific Tissue (one of two women directors); and many other firsts in her 28-year career in the paper industry. Her secrets to success focus on the principles and habits needed to succeed in business and personal life. While the events are told with humor, the journey was not always easy but certainly fulfilling and full of memories.

Versie teaches how to defy the odds and make a positive difference at home, in the office, in the classroom, or in the community.

By internalizing these principles, you can overcome barriers of achievement and reach beyond your limits to the fulfillment of larger goals.

Versie is a graduate of Alabama State University with a B.S. in Chemistry and Math. In her 28 year career she has worked for several of the paper giants; SCA Tissue North America, Georgia Pacific, Wisconsin Tissue-Chesapeake, and Scott Paper/ S.D.Warren Division. Versie has served on the board of several professional, civic and cultural organizations - IFMA (International Foodservice Manufacturers Association); SafeHome, a shelter for women and children from domestic abuse. She currently serves on the board of The Walter L. Kimbrough Leadership Institute, and Black Technology Corporation. Versie is the mother of one daughter, Valerie. She likes to travel, play golf, read, network and spend time with family and friends.

Contributions

Choose Your Shoes...Then Take a Walk

ORDER FORM

You can order **Choose Your Shoes...Then Take a Walk** by Versie M. Black from your local bookstore by supplying them with the ISBN: 0-9729138-0-7 (Trade paperback $12.95), or personalized autographed copies direct from the author via mail at:

Versie Consulting, P.O. Box 724495 Atlanta, GA 31139

Author, Versie Black, is available for interviews and as a guest speaker on the topics of sales strategies, empowerment, personal motivation, self-help, or developing effective personal and professional relationships. Address email inquires and replies to **vmbda1@msn.com** or **www.VersieConsulting.com.**

Please send me _____ copies of Versie M. Black's
Choose Your Shoes...Then Take a Walk @ $12.95 each, plus 5% sales tax (0.65)= total $13.60. Add $4.00 postage and handling, and $2.00 for each additional copy in the same order.

Please include complete mailing address and allow two weeks for delivery. Your order will receive our prompt attention.

Name_____

Address _____

City_____ ST_____Zip_____

Phone_____

E-Mail_____